May, 2018
To all who read this:
May you be reminded
of the power
of love!
♡ J Kint S. H——

Love Wins

is dedicated to:
My children, Elijah & Penelope.
May the truth of your worth speak louder
than the lies of this world. Live loved!

Written by Kimby Shult Hughes
Illustrated by Tess McCulloch

Special thanks to:

The African American Studies professors, ministers, and friends
who spoke truth to me with love and without judgment.
In doing so, you helped me better understand my privilege
and taught me how to approach the world with more awareness.

I still have much to learn. I remain grateful for
those who are wise enough to challenge distorted world views,
thoughtful enough to hold a space for tough conversations,
and courageous enough to speak vulnerably
about their own experiences.

"The rock in the water does not know the pain of the rock in the sun."
~Haitian Proverb

There were some kids who sat upon
the same earth side by side.
Some were in the water...

Life was pretty comfortable
for the kids playing in the water.
The sun would shine on them
but never would they get hotter.

Life wasn't quite as easy
for the kids out in the sun.
The sun's hot rays were exhausting
by the time the day was done.

The kids within the water
were as comfortable as could be.
They simply did not think about
the kids out in the heat.

The kids on the land watched
those in the water every day.
With heavy hearts they wondered
why they weren't allowed to play.

The kids in the heat simply wanted
to be seen, heard, and known.
But the other kids ignored them,
leaving them all alone.

It was only when they stopped to look
that the kids in the water did see
the kids standing on hot land
whose lives were not as easy.

With an act of awareness and love,
a kid from the water extended her hand.
It was a powerful gesture, filled with hope.
One through which healing began.

It is love that wins in the end.
If we open our hearts we can be,
children playing side by side
in a world filled with hope and peace.

73617840R00015

Made in the USA
San Bernardino, CA
11 April 2018